Mental Warmups
FOR THE Choral Director

by LLOYD PFAUTSCH

GEORGE MARTIN

Mental Warmups
FOR THE Choral Director
by LLOYD PFAUTSCH

LAWSON-GOULD music publishers, inc.
609 FIFTH AVENUE, NEW YORK, N.Y. 10017
G. SCHIRMER, INC., sole selling representatives

L.G.Co.51474

Contents

Let's Warm Up

Do choral conductors ever "warm up"? If so, how? If not, why not?

Baseball pitchers "loosen up" in the bullpen before taking the mound.

Football players "get the kinks out" before lining up.

Golfers chip, putt, and take practice swings before teeing off.

Basketball players go through the ritual of outside shots, layups, and free throws before the whistle blows.

String players work the bow arm and the fingers of the left hand long before an orchestral rehearsal begins.

Brass and woodwind players prepare their lips and check their embouchure and breath control well in advance of a conductor's downbeat.

While singers have been using their vocal equipment for variable amounts of time prior to a choral rehearsal, it helps the vocal mechanism to "vocalize" before engaging in the rigors of a rehearsal.

But what does the choral conductor do? What can he do? What should he do BEFORE a rehearsal?

I hope that what follows will be thought-provoking to the readers as they prepare to conduct a chorus. Thus, they are "mental warmups," with aphoristic intentions.

*For the five who have accepted and
endured my devotion to
the choral art.*

Conductors Move In Mysterious Ways

Conducting involves the transfer of spiritual, musical, and emotional impulses from the conductor to the chorus.

Conducting involves communication. It could be called musical semaphore. Messages are sent to the chorus which tell the singers what they should do and when they should do what the conductor and the score demand. It has been said that conducting is like choreography; the movements of many conductors underscore that statement. However, there is a very subtle difference. In dance, the movements are made WITH the music and the music actuates the dance. In conducting, the movements must be carefully timed so that they PRECEDE the music, since the conducting gestures actuate the music.

Choral performance is essentially concerted or communal. It requires the interaction and interdependence of the conductor and the chorus, the various sections within a chorus, the personnel within these various sections, the composer and the conductor-chorus liaison, the composer-conductor-chorus liaison and the audience.

What you are "saying to a chorus" with your face and eyes is frequently much more important than how you are moving your arms and hands. However, if your arm and hand movements are incongruous with what your face and eyes are communicating, the chorus can be distracted by these movements and thus the effect of your face and your eyes will be far less than its potential.

So much time is spent on musical and technical preparation for conducting that a most important factor is generally overlooked or assumed — the physical preparation. Every conductor should work seriously on maintaining good muscle tone. This concern should not be limited only to those muscles involved or employed in conducting. Every conductor should have a regular routine for exercising daily. Special emphasis should be placed on exercises for the legs, back, shoulders, and arms. However, it is advisable to check with your physician concerning the extent, frequency, and type of exercises to employ.

Many maintain that conducting cannot be taught, that formal and harmonic analysis of scores provides a conductor with all of the knowledge he needs in order to conduct. Analytical ability, its development, and its refinement are certainly important. But, using the same rationale, all one would need to do to play the piano, organ, or any other instrument would be to study the available literature for that instrument. The necessary technique involved in actual performance could be bypassed. Of course, this is ridiculous. Many long hours are spent developing technical mastery of the individual instruments. But not so with conducting. There is a "language" involved in conducting which must be learned to enable the conductor to communicate with his choral group. This "language" enables a conductor to transfer the knowledge he acquires through analysis and training. If he cannot communicate, his knowledge and musical training are of relative value.

The beating of time in a clear pattern is merely elemental. All of conducting technique is actually subservient to what is ultimately significant. Since conducting involves communication, a conductor must have something "to say" to the group and it must "be said" in an engaging way. It is distressing to see conductors who are good musicians (have something to say) but who are bad conductors (do not speak the language) It is even more distressing to see conductors who have mastered the movements and procedures (know the language) but merely expose their shallow musicianship (have nothing of consequence to say).

With the impetuosity of youth, too many students want to conduct ensembles before they have experienced the disciplines and artistic demands of individual performance, regardless of the performing medium. Conducting, like composition, has been elevated to an exalted position by these many students who consider personal performance too mundane, even unnecessary.

The purely mechanical function of a conductor — namely beating time — although essential, is strictly elementary, merely a base of operation and a point of departure. But it is as basic and as important to a conductor as fingering technique is to any instrumentalist. Some conductors never get beyond this "base" while others consider such concern to be beneath their dignity. Both groups are incomplete conductors.

The success of every choral conductor depends upon craftsmanship. The craftsmanship of one conductor may be part of his creative endowment which he develops, refines, and masters. The craftsmanship of another may not be a part of his creative endowment but the result of imitation and/or emulation. The former conductor is like Michelangelo who used his craftsmanship to expose the forms which he saw held within a block of marble. He uses his craftsmanship to reproduce the sounds he hears when he reads a score. The latter conductor is like the "Sunday painter" who learns his art by copying masterworks. This conductor borrows the craftsmanship of others in an attempt to reproduce the sounds he hears when the others conduct. In between these extremes are countless variations.

Conductors should always convey to the performing ensemble the underlying subdivision of the basic beats. In a very subtle way their gestures should enable the chorus to feel kinesthetically the "life pulse" of the music.

The basic skills or rudimentary techniques involved in conducting can be taught, to anyone by a reasonably competent teacher, but not the art of conducting. Mastery of this art separates the gifted conductor from the pedestrian conductor. Yet this mastery is not achieved without the basic skills, without the spark of temperament, without convincing communication, and without contagious dedication to the score at hand.

While the basic fundamentals of conducting technique are essential for the success of any conductor, they must ultimately be subservient to the music being conducted. They lose their mechanical meaning as they become related to the tempo, dynamics, nuance, phrasing, etc.

The "born" conductor assimilates the craftsmanship of conducting as easily and as quickly as a foreign language is mastered by a person who has been given an "ear" for languages, or as any professional discipline is appropriated by a person who has a natural propensity for that discipline.

There is no canon or Biblical justification or rational explanation as to why one should never conduct with the left hand. Do any of the following ever use their left hand in carrying out their separate responsibilites within their professions: baseball players, golfers, tennis players, or a person who writes? Southpaws have always been welcome in baseball especially at first base, and the eternal search goes on for another Musial or Williams. For years, left handed golf clubs were rare. Consider the number of grade school teachers who have worked so diligently to help students learn how to write right (handed). Have you ever noticed how many air line employees write with their left hand when they prepare air travel tickets? However, since this is a "musical" consideration let me employ a prime musical example. I once had the privilege of participating in a three-hour rehearsal of the NBC Symphony Orchestra and Chorus under the direction of Arturo Toscanini. Toscanini conducted the whole rehearsal LEFT HANDED because bursitis made it impossible for him to move his right arm. I did not hear one member of the orchestra say: "Maestro, we cannot follow your beat because you are using your left hand" or "Doesn't he know that you are not supposed to conduct with your left arm?" The rehearsal had its usual excitement and refinements. Toscanini did not appear to be inhibited in any way. He worked as he always did and communicated as effectively as he always communicated, only this time with his LEFT ARM!

Expansion of conducting technique with confident mastery will always facilitate the transfer of inner musical feeling and understanding. But the conductor who concentrates on technique for the sake of technique (and not as a means to an end) will limit his choir to seeing "through a glass darkly" or, perhaps, even to seeing that there is little or nothing behind the glass.

The most effective choral conductors are those who possess technical ability or craftsmanship and profound musicality in a balanced relationship.

Self-conscious conducting is to be avoided as rigorously as self-conscious singing, speaking, acting, lecturing, and preaching. Conducting must always be subordinate to the musical demands of the score.

A choral conductor should "lose himself" in his work with a sense of dedication and a level of enthusiasm that is highly contagious.

A conductor must present to a chorus a personification of the work to be performed. All that he does, all that he says, every look, gesture, and word, even the pace and dynamic level of his speaking, must be related to the composition and reflect its purpose, content, and creator. One of the most difficult responsibilities any conductor faces is faithfulness to the composer's ideas as expressed through the symbols on a page of music.

A choral conductor should operate like a highly successful salesman who concentrates on selling his product rather than selling himself.

Enthusiasm, showmanship, or even formal, theoretical, or stylistic understanding of musical materials will never obviate craftsmanship in conducting. Have you ever heard or seen a recognized artist who has not mastered the craftsmanship involved in his performing medium? Indeed, it is the craftsmanship that has made possible the release and the sharing of that which separates the artist from the sciolist. Many young conductors fail to comprehend the importance of craftsmanship and avoid its inherent disciplines and advantages until recurrent failures force an objective re-appraisal of their conducting technique. I have seen many young conductors who were released for uninhibited communication and for maturation when they accepted the importance and necessity of craftsmanship. The craftsmanship of conducting is as helpful and as necessary for a conductor as mastery of a foreign language is for a diplomat.

It is difficult to understand choral conductors who permit accompanists and soloists to have free rein in performance. They let the accompanist determine the tempo of introductions and interludes. They let soloists "interpret" according to their "feelings." They forget that a choral conductor is responsible for the WHOLE performance and not just the measures during which the chorus sings. The accompanists and soloists should follow the conductor, and his control and guidance must be empathetic, not tyrannical.

Any choral group can sing and perform without a conductor. But a choral conductor is musically impotent without a group of singers — he cannot perform choral music without the performing instrument: the choir. Generally speaking, a choral group will sing more effectively and efficiently under a conductor, although some choral performances would radically contradict this statement. Moral: Do not speak about "my" choir. Resist reporting on what "I" do chorally. The plural pronoun is not only preferred, it is also more honest and factual.

Instrumentalists and vocalists can practice in solitude, but not the conductor. Of course, he can work on control of beat patterns, expressive gestures, etc., by himself but he must relate all of this to the sound of his "instrument," the choral ensemble, which can only be experienced in the rehearsal. Thus, the choir participates in the choral conductor's practicing since he needs the response of voices just as the organist needs the response of the organ and the pianist the response of the piano. Bruno Walter has pointed out that all conductors are consequently not able to begin their professional careers with the same security, assurance, or technical proficiency that other performing musicians acquire as background.*

You must learn to hear what is actually being produced and not what you are expecting to hear or what you want to hear. Conductors can be easily fooled if they are not careful; they can lose a necessary objectivity which is required for a

*Bruno Walter, *Of Music and Music-Making* (New York, 1961), p. 84.

correct appraisal of the sound a chorus is producing. It takes a few years before a young conductor is freed from the concern about what he is *doing* so that he can be concerned about what he is *hearing*. It takes a longer time for his powers of judgment to be related to the sounds he hears in his inner ear. Before he is able to do the latter, he must understand that what he is hearing is related to what he is doing.

When he conducts, a choral conductor must depend on his ear and arm in that sequence. He must hear in his "inner ear" the sounds he wants the choir to produce, and his arm then moves to elicit that response from the singers. His "other ear" then reports to him whether or not he has been successful. If not successful, he must then analyze and evaluate the arm movements objectively.

A choral conductor must listen to his choir to determine if he is hearing an "instant replay" of what he expected to hear.

Controlling the dynamic gradations in choral performance is exceedingly difficult. The conductor can demonstrate by personal example when he tempers the dynamic levels of his own vocal production. The chorus can imitate and approximate what it hears, but ultimate control rests within the conductor's conducting technique. He cannot control the chorus as easily as he can his own voice. He runs the constant danger of asking for too much or too little too soon or too late, of collective impetuosity or reticence, and of misjudging the acoustical properties of various concert halls. Only experience will teach him how to circumvent such hazards. Of all performers, the conductor is the only one who does not have direct control over his "instrument."

A chorus of voices, the choral conductor's "instrument," cannot be controlled in the same way as an instrumentalist controls the sound of his instrument. The chorus is much more delicate, inconsistent, and unpredictable. As a result, much of what a conductor must do suggests hypnotic control.

A conductor's musicality will be partially exposed through his establishment, control, shaping, and maintenance of tempo and rhythmic flow as he conducts.

Conducting in performance is primarily a supportive action in that most of the responsibilities of the conductor should have been taken care of in the preceding rehearsals. What a conductor does during a performance should merely remind the chorus of what he had asked them to do during rehearsals.

Every choral conductor should acquaint himself with the problems and responsibilities of working with instrumental ensembles. At best, his knowledge will be peripheral. Yet, if he is a disciplined craftsman as he conducts and uses his craftsmanship to share his understanding of the score, the instrumentalists will respond to his leadership.

To conduct from memory or not to conduct from memory, that is a repeated question. Some conductors have photographic memories — one look at a score and the negative is always there for reproduction. Some conductors have a memory potential that results from lengthy exposure to or repeated performances of a score. Other conductors have difficulty remembering that they should look at the score to be reminded of what they must do. Still others look constantly at the score for fear that they will lose their contact with the music. And the older we grow, the more difficult it is for memory to operate. Moral: Remember what you can remember, but neither overestimate nor underestimate your potential.

In a rehearsal or performance, a choir should never feel that they are being led by the conductor. Rather they should feel that they are being freed to respond to the musical stimuli and in that response to re-create with collective empathy. This sense of having contributed to or participated in an approximation of the composer's intentions is a satisfaction that exceeds the adulation of an audience. Never deprive your singers of this experience. When you do you limit your own satisfactions as a conductor.

Have you ever noticed how closely a choir watches the conductor when they are singing from memory? But what are they watching? Too often, they are watching a conductor who is looking at HIS music. There is something incongruous about a conductor using music when a choir is singing without music. I usually work in the opposite manner. And I have always been able to get my groups to watch me even though they use music.

Most people in an audience tend to *watch* a conductor instead of listening to the performers in a chorus. They also tend to base their critical reactions on what they see or on how the conductor "looks" as he conducts. The extent of their understanding is, at best, that of a dilettante.

One never ceases to learn more about conducting if one is alert, analytical, concerned about the depths of musical understanding, has the capacity for growth, and has an interest in change or variation. Conducting is a difficult and demanding art, and, as Richard Strauss has pointed out, advancing years help the individual conductor to realize this. Only the youthful are convinced that "anyone can conduct" (also many administrators).

Every conductor is tempted to conclude that the performance revolves around him, that he is the most important ingredient, that he must dominate, control, and shape the musical performance. The egocentric conductor never understands the contributory role of the composer and performers. Because his sense of importance is excessive and unwarranted, there is inevitably a sameness about the performances which does not emphasize the music and which reflects on him as a conductor.

A conductor must never come between the chorus and the audience. His actions as a conductor must never be distracting, never call attention to himself, and never be excessive. Many conductors conduct as if they were moving their arms for the benefit of the audience rather than the singers. This is choreography on the podium and is not conducting. It is preoccupation with the self and not with the music.

Too many choral conductors employ conducting mannerisms which seem intent on leading people in an audience to comment: "He certainly works hard to get what he wants from his choir." What the audience does not realize is that if the conductor has to work that hard in a performance he has failed to work hard enough in the rehearsals. The professional observer is not fooled by what he sees, for what he hears is much more revealing.

Ultimately, all conductors are confronted by this humbling fact: the more effectively one conducts, the less one's conducting is necessary. Thus a conductor is like a teacher. He can work with his group in such a way that they become increasingly dependent on him, or he can work with them in such a way that they become increasingly independent of him. Naturally, a conductor will always have pertinence as a focal point, a guide or source of reminders in performance, plus providing new motivations. However, when you relate this posture to what a conductor does in rehearsals, his significance in performance is somewhat negligible.

The choral art is done a great disservice when the conductor is featured instead of the collective efforts of composer, choir, and conductor.

Many conductors limit their conducting gestures to the point where they seem to be hiding the fact that they are conducting. Others are so flamboyant in their conducting that they seem to be trying to prove that they are conducting. Both groups betray servility to the audience rather than to the art.

Conducting posture and mannerisms are frequently obsessions and, for these conductors, attest to the pre-eminence of sight over sound. Seeing is believing for many people. A good conductor will always be more concerned about doing what he needs to do to obtain the performance standards he respects than he will be about a Hollywood appearance on the podium.

Conducting affectations are in themselves of questionable merit, especially when the affectations assume ascendancy over the music and its demands on the conductor. When these affectations are propagated either through imitation or pedagogy, integrity is supplanted by duplicity.

A choral conductor should always maintain a personal, professional and pedagogical detachment from his chorus. This will allow for critical discrimination and appraisal, minimize the danger of addiction to the same sounds, permit consideration of the comparable and competitive, encourage recognition of the exemplary, and make possible continued development, enrichment, and refinement.

A choral contest is frequently an anathema. The conductor must receive a judgment he would rather avoid and the judge must make a judgment he would rather avoid. And usually the conductor thinks that he would make the better judge while the judge thinks that he would make the better conductor. How many times has neither been correct in his assumption?

A poor or weak choral conductor can fool some of the singers throughout any rehearsal. He can fool all of the singers during parts of a rehearsal. But a good or competent choral conductor does not need to fool any of the singers in any rehearsal. Singers almost instinctively react favorably to vocal and choral competency.

If your enthusiasm for the choral art should ever wane, seek out another profession immediately. Perfunctory choral conducting produces prosaic choral sounds.

The good conductor stimulates. The bad conductor stultifies.

Our Instrument: The Voice En Masse

A choral conductor will never know enough about the human voice; even the collective understanding of those at work in the profession is incomplete.

A choir will sing as its conductor conducts and will reflect the conductor's technique — good or bad.

A choir will sing as its conductor sings or as he would sing if he could or as he was taught to sing when he sang under another conductor; a choir frequently sounds like the conductor's voice multiplied by the total of the personnel . . . . good, bad or indifferent.

The singer is the most maligned of all musicians. It is trite to say: "There are singers and there are musicians" or, "Singers seem to have resonance where their brains ought to be." But every conductor should THINK like a singer and work like a singer. Toscanini used to plead with his players to "sing." Many principal performers in symphonies talk about the importance of listening to recordings of the best singers and learning from them about the contour of phrasing. However, I believe that to conduct singers, you have to understand thoroughly all that is involved in vocal production, and whatever you do must assist and not frustrate the singers.

Never ask your singers to sing in any manner contrary to what you KNOW (or should know) is correct. I am not speaking about the occasional affectation or purposeful distortion; I am concerned about the normal, regular, prevalent type of production. To do otherwise is to encourage faulty production, bad habits, and ruined voices. Do not tamper with the God-given instrument.

In helping a chorus sing correctly — "corny" as it may sound — an ounce of demonstration is worth a pound of explanation. But the demonstration must be good.

Never superimpose or force the sound of your own voice on a chorus. Who wants to hear a soprano section that sounds like a group of lady basses in a high register? Let the sections sound like themselves: sopranos, altos, tenors, and basses, who are approximating your good vocal technique (provided it can be classified as "good").

The conductor must help the singers breathe, and the gesture employed must convey to the singers the following:
1) the precise moment for the start of inhalation;
2) the extent or capacity of the inhalation;
3) the dynamic intensity to be involved in the subsequent phonation;
and all of this must be done in relationship to the rhythmic pulse. Breathing must be related to tempo and dynamics. It must never be begun too early or too late and must be neither excessively expansive nor shallow!

Relax! Tell your singers to relax. How many times have you heard this and said this? For many singers, teachers of singing, and choral conductors this statement is almost a motto. Do it! Relax completely — and you will fall over! What we want to get rid of is EXCESSIVE and UNNECESSARY tension. Moral: Ask and it might be given unto you. But know what you are asking for and why.

I once heard a famous symphony orchestra conductor comment on a recording by a superior university choral

group. He said, "They do not sound as mature as
.... (naming a professional choral organization). Although this man deserved
the respect he commanded as an orchestral conductor, he
exposed a novice's understanding of the choral ensemble.
Of course the university choral group did not sound as
mature as the professionals but he had no right to expect
them to do so. What university orchestra plays with the
maturity of a professional symphony? What university
football team expects to match professional quality? Professionals are a selected group, made up of the best from
university organizations and other centers of "minor
league" training. Unfortunately, this is not an isolated
instance of such misunderstanding as far as choral performances are concerned.

In choral or solo singing, all nuances, dynamics, crescendi,
diminuendi, etc., must be ordered and controlled with
restraint.

To compare the human voice with a flute, violin, or
any other man-made instrument is an insult to the God-given
instrument which is always more distinctive than what is
man-made.

One of the most difficult vocal disciplines to develop in
any choral group is the all-important ability to sustain a
melodic line and support it with the vital intensity and
expansiveness required for the note values within the
line. A conductor can assist the singers by the type of
tension he employs in his conducting gestures and the
manner in which he moves from one beat to the next.

Never force the voices of your singers at any stage of
their development. Never permit or encourage an emotional projection as a substitution for technical control
or as a coverup for technical inadequacies.

No amount of study of music literature, music theory, voice, conducting, etc., will ever supplant the importance and value of experience gained through vocal ensemble participation and "standing in front of your own chorus." Moral: All theory without practice makes Jack a poor conductor.

Where is a singer going to learn to sight sing? Where will he learn the disciplines of vocal ensemble? Where will he learn that God created good voices other than his own? Where will he learn that the vocal world does not revolve around him? Where can he put into practice "under fire" the vocal disciplines developing in the private studio? Answer: In a choral rehearsal.

There are a number of vocal and choral effects: the hum and *bocca chiusa* or *bouche fermée.* However, it must be remembered that these are merely "effects" that provide variety when used sparingly. Some voice teachers and conductors who have been influenced by teachers who stress affected production make the mistake of creating a norm out of the effect. Thus, one hears some choirs always sing with an overemphasis on head resonance while others always sing with a "smiling face." Right? Wrong! Wrong? Right!

Most people tend to sing as they speak. All of the bad habits and regional colloquialisms heard in speech become accentuated when prolonged in singing. The old Italian maxim, "Sing as you speak" can be most dangerous.

"You must overpronounce when you sing" is a diplomatic way of telling your singers to speak correctly.

As a choral conductor, you will have to spend much of your rehearsal time working on English diction. Actually, you will be the chief disciplinarian in this area. You will exert the greatest influence on the singers in behalf of good diction. The responsibility is yours because the private voice teacher either assumes his student has a mastery of English or merely provides token guidance. Voice pedagogical tradition in America dictates an "accepted" sequence of language study, i.e., Italian, German, and French, with the last two frequently exchanging positions. Why waste time on English in the voice studio?

Many voice teachers contend that "English is an ungrateful language for singing." Do not assist the propagation of this fallacy. It may be more complicated than Italian but it *is* a singable language. The root of the problem is bad English. It is no more difficult than any other language if you form vowels *correctly* and articulate consonants *correctly*.

It is not surprising that vocalists have difficulty singing English and that many contemporary composers have difficulty setting the English language. Consider how we Americans speak and how our interest has waned in elocution. Refined, poetic speech is considered an affectation. The composer not only participates in this posture; his setting of prosody reflects this posture. Then, too, the miniature or diminutive form of composition is out of style, since society is impressed more by the expansiveness of music rather than by what it is communicating.

I am always amused by Europeans who smile knowingly when Americans "attempt to sing" (or speak) French, German, or Italian because they never suspect that their English diction is less than equally poor! I will never forget hearing a Viennese chorus perform the Brahms *Liebeslieder Waltzes* in English. What incongruity! What ludicrous English diction!

There are voice teachers who do not allow their students to sing in choral ensembles (except, of course, opera choruses). They might "hurt" their voices! Choral singing is bad for the solo voice. They should "save" their voices! True, there are some choral conductors who demand a vocal production alien to the vocal studio and injurious to the voice. But the many charlatans in the vocal studios are usually the loudest in berating choral singing while protecting their "method." If the individual singer is receiving competent pedagogy in the private studio, singing in a choral group under a good choral conductor will help rather than hinder vocal development. Moral: You can still fool some of the students much of the time.

The goal of most vocal pedagogy is the operatic stage, hence the emphasis on the mastery of foreign languages rather than on the mastery of English. Additional emphasis is placed on the size of sound rather than vocal artistry. Impresarios and concert series provide the public with recitals by "name singers" who temporarily leave the operatic stage for an evening of song with their admirers. When they sing arias they are convincing recitalists, but conventional programming always includes German lieder, French chanson, and songs in English. During these groups of songs most of these singers merely expose the size of their voices.

Opera invloves an essentially intimate experience. When so treated, the orchestral forces are significant yet partially subservient so that the human voice can function without forcing or "projecting." However, today, we need binoculars and microphones to see and hear. This detachment has led to disenchantment with opera as an art form, although it struggles on as a social activity. One wonders how long opera will continue as a spectacle since it has abrogated the original intention of lyric theater.

When choruses appear in opera, at least two of the following postures are operational: 1) the chorus is given static staging so that the ensemble sound can be heard; 2) the chorus is mobile with staging superseding sound; 3) the choristers seem to be contending with each other to prove that the wrong singers are singing the leading roles. The instance of superlative choral work is so rare that it arouses an ovational response when realized.

Many choral conductors work on intonation as if it were only a tonal or intervallic problem. They rarely realize that ·improper vowel formations contribute to the primary problem. Collective production of correct vowel formations will almost invariably result in good intonation, assuming that the singers approximate the correct pitches.

Is perfect pitch necessary? My friends with perfect pitch answer: "No, it is a hindrance." Yet, I have observed them using this gift to great advantage and admit I was guilty of envy. However, I have also observed other conductors not so endowed work most effectively (even just as effectively) using their ears, which they were always developing in terms of greater musical and technical (vocal) sensitivity. Moral: Let him who has ears to hear use them according to the potential of his endowment.

Every choral conductor should assist the regimen of private vocal study by helping the singers to exercise the proper singing muscles with vigor and regularity.

One of the main reasons for the variance of the choral sounds produced by choral groups of different nationalities is the relation of that sound to the native language and the way the vocal mechanism is used to produce that language. Significant factors are the length of the vowel sounds, their resonance potential, and the intensity of consonant articulation in the spoken language which conditions the muscular action involved and thus helps determine the nature and quality of the sung word.

Most vocal pedagogy involves the elimination of bad habits.

These habits will be complex and diverse in direct relation to the number of singers comprising a choral ensemble. Yet, singing in a chorus under a choral conductor who is capable of providing group vocal therapy can make an invaluable contribution toward eliminating bad habits in singing.

No individual choral member should ever be expected to learn how to use his voice by listening to the sounds of the conductor's voice, the sounds of the section in which he sings, or the sounds of the group itself. He should learn mostly from the sensations of greater freedom, correctness, and "ring" in his own voice as he is encouraged to use it properly under a competent choral conductor. It has often been said that there are solo voices and choral voices. This is ridiculous. Certainly, not every singer is good enough to sing solos but no soloist is too good to sing in a chorus. Correct singing is correct singing whether in a solo or an ensemble performance.

Although it is always painful to hear a choral group sing with poor or improper technique, it is shocking when one reflects on what has been happening to these voices during the numerous rehearsals prior to the performance.

Are You Rehearsing More
But Enjoying It Less?

A good stage demeanor requires preparation and discipline. Remember that a choir is seen before it is heard.

The choral conductor who is easily satisfied with choral efforts will always become more easily satisfied.

Develop your ear so that you will not only hear faulty intonation, incorrect vowel and consonant production, improper balance of parts and all of the other choral "problems" but also so that you will be able to detect the causes. Much rehearsal time is lost by conductors who, failing to hear the causes when they hear the "problems," waste time searching for the causes and/or corrections. Immediate diagnosis followed by ready prescriptions is to be desired.

Part of a conductor's growth and development should involve the following sequence of experiences:
   A. Realization of mistakes
   B. Acceptance of mistakes
   C. Analysis of mistakes
   D. Correction of mistakes
   E. Learning from mistakes
   A. Recognition of additional mistakes and/or new mistakes followed by B, C, D, E, A, etc, thus repeating the cycle ad infinitum.

Do you know how to pace *yourself* in a rehearsal? Are you exhausted physically, mentally, emotionally, and musically at the end of a rehearsal or earlier? It could be the result of the pace at which you rehearse. To avoid this, you must learn to work within a balanced relationship between tension and relaxation.

The earlier in your choral conducting career you learn not to waste rehearsal time the more you will be able to accomplish.

In rehearsing, technical disciplines must never be ends in themselves. The conductor must employ these disciplines in the service of more effective and artistic performances. Some conductors depend solely on emotional or spiritual inspiration to elevate the performance standards, and others on technical disciplines. To stress either to the neglect of the other limits the level of attainment. However, to stress both in proper balance has an unlimited potential.

All choral groups should develop a sensitivity for balance of voice parts. While the conductor should exercise ultimate control over balance and assist its constancy when he conducts, all singers should be taught to listen to parts other than their own, to have a sensitivity toward the relative importance of their contribution to chordal structure, verbal nuance, and dynamic stress, to know how to control ascending and descending intervals, and to understand the variable demands involved throughout the range of their part. But even with all of this understanding, the singers will be dependent on the conductor for subtle adjustments. Without this understanding, the conductor usually ends up being satisfied with mediocrity.

When you share with a choir for the first time any music which you have previously performed, you will find your patience tested. Remember that you also looked at this music for the first time. Do not forget how long it took you to master the intricacies of the demands of the particular composition.

Whenever a chorus performs in public, what the audience hears is not so much the result of what the conductor is doing by way of communicative gesture while on the podium but rather the result of what he has done during the weeks of rehearsal prior to the performance. Yet his skill in reminding the chorus of what he had required in rehearsal will separate that type of performance which suggests the singing of zombies from that type which suggests interdependence and corporate re-creation of the music.

Too many young conductors confuse temperament with emotional outbursts. It is generally believed that temperament and genius are interrelated, especially in the arts (there is a common misunderstanding that all artists are "temperamental"). Like the art of conducting, temperament cannot be taught but must be part of one's native endowment. How a conductor uses this temperament is even more significant than the fact that he possesses it.

Singing with your choir in rehearsal can be hazardous. Everyone does this and necessarily so, but you should realize that it can become a habit which is difficult to break. Constant singing with the chorus limits and dulls aural perception.

When a choir has its music memorized it can "give" more in performance (whatever that may mean). I do not believe this. As many mistakes occur during memorized performances as during those given with music. My experience has been that there are fewer mistakes with music. And a great danger in stressing memorization is that "canned" performances are an end product. So much rehearsal time is spent on memorization by overdoing countless repetitions that actual performances lack spontaneity and sound "stale." What instrumental groups play from memory? And they do not have words to recall (although you could argue that words help memory of music, and rightly so). However, emphasis on memorization of music in performance is relatively recent in the history of music.

Most members of amateur choral organizations attend rehearsals in order to sing. They do not come for lectures, reminiscences — to hear you talk! Though you may be witty, informative, and engaging, your job is to rehearse. Advancing age and experience seem to encourage verbosity. While you may have more to say, and what you say may have more significance as you grow older, age and experience should help you know when and why you should speak. It should also help you know when not to speak and what not to say.

Women singers have a strange proclivity for assuming that cutoffs are cues to start talking.

All verbal directions should be given quickly, explicitly, and decisively. He who hesitates loses not only the attention of the group but also the dynamic momentum of the rehearsal, assuming that there had been a dynamic momentum.

Once a chorus has some acquaintance with the entire composition, spend your valuable rehearsal time on those sections that involve the greatest technical and musical problems. Regular review of what is easy wastes rehearsal time.

When rehearsing, one of the unpardonable sins is wasting time. Every minute is precious and should not be abused. The conductor should never permit any member of the chorus to waste any rehearsal time and he himself should strive to avoid being guilty of the same thing. This is not just the exact amount of time that is wasted according to the minute and second, but this amount of time must be multiplied by the number of people involved in a rehearsal thus representing the total amount of time lost and wasted. The conductor is responsible for saving time through the proper use of time. Part of his job is to see that the limited rehearsal time is utilized with expeditious care. He must "save time" for the group.

A choral conductor, desiring more vocal intensity, shouted: "Sing lustfully!" Moral: All choral conductors are occasionally afflicted with "foot in mouth" disease, which is rarely fatal.

How did you like to be treated by the choral conductors under whom you sang? Recall the old admonition: he who would be master must first be slave.

Beware of impetuosity, pomposity, and verbosity.

A chorus can be likened to a young child. To grow and develop, it needs a balanced diet (repertoire), the right combination of love and discipline (praise and criticism), educational guidance (the tools of musicianship, e.g. sight--singing and reading), social guidance (reciprocal respect and responsibility), encouragement and restraint (the increasingly difficult challenge of new repertoire but not too soon), the satisfactions of accomplishment (good performances within capabilities), the leavening experience of failure (the freedom to err, though hopefully in rehearsal and without constant chastening), and to be on its own (know the importance of individual responsibility).

They Wrote It; We Sing It

Today competent composers of choral music are almost as rare as competent writers of lyric poetry.

There is a difference between vocal and instrumental melodic lines. A choral conductor must be able to know and hear this difference. When the melodic line is graciously vocal, he must know how to help the singers take advantage of the composer's vocal sensitivity. When the melodic line is instrumental, he must know how to help the singers counteract the encumbrances provided by the composer.

Vocal and choral music is (or should be) essentially logo-genic. A choral composition could be called a musical exegesis of a text with the vocal lines, dynamic levels, harmonic scheme and rhythm, note relationships, etc., all being consistent with syllabic nuance, prosody, etc. Serial composition for the chorus is anti-vocal since its genus is the preconceived sequence of intervals to which the text must conform even though syllabic nuance, duration, and rhythm may contradict speech norms. Here a composition device assumes ascendency over the main purpose of vocal music in the germinative sense, i.e. a logogenic basis. A composer, of course, has the right to use serial technique and to use it purposefully in his vocal and choral compositions. But it is usually only an interesting experiment that treats the voice like an instrument, the text like a vestigial remnant, and the device like a god. Its purpose is not to serve the performing medium but rather to exercise the mind, tantalize the eye, and test or defy the ear but without the usual sensory satisfactions. I will not bother to elaborate on the lack of satisfaction for the singers and the audience.

It is important that a choral conductor develop as early as possible in his career the ability to look at a score and internally hear its sounds. Rehearsing then involves the ritual of attempting to obtain from a chorus an approximation of that internal sound, a process that can be as satisfying as it can be frustrating depending upon the conductor's ability to communicate, inspire, refine, and persevere.

Too many composers today are instrumentally oriented. They do not know how to write for the voice, or how to use the voice (though they can abuse it); they are callous toward vocal limitations and are oblivious to the problems of vowels and consonants; in short, they do not show the voice the same respect they have for any man-made instrument.

I heard an eminent composer state that you could always tell if a composer was a pianist by the way he wrote for the piano, especially in his songs. I was young at the time, and because of timidity (which I mistook for respect) I did not say what I was thinking: "You can also tell if the composer is a singer or has done much singing by the way he writes for the voice or chorus." Writing as a singer, once you have experienced the satisfactions and ease involved in singing songs which are sensitive to the human instrument, you are made even more aware of poor vocal and choral writing.

A difficult and demanding choral work written by a composer who understands and respects the vocal and choral potential and/or limitations will always be easier to prepare and perform than the easiest choral work written by a composer who has no understanding of or respect for the human instrument. The latter's choral efforts are invariably difficult because they are anti-vocal.

There is constant lamentation over the lack of significant new operas. There are many reasons given, such as costs involved, danger of limited box office appeal, etc. But, one of the main reasons is the composer's inability to write convincingly for the human voice, because he is not facile in writing for the solo singer or for the unaccompanied chorus. Most composers employ instrumental devices or techniques in writing for the voice and it does not work. Anyone who has sung Bach and Handel understands this difference, especially in the vocal solos. Composers should study Handel and consider how he wrote for the voice. They should also look at Schumann's lieder.

The interpretive role of the conductor is often misunderstood and frequently overemphasized. Interpretation does not involve license to improvise on the musical ingredients provided by the composer. But interpretation does involve: 1) an earnest attempt to discover and understand the composer's original intentions; 2) the artistic realization of the printed page to which the conductor and chorus contribute through their technical competency their personal dimensions of discovery and understanding. The composer himself actually contributes to that understanding and discovery when he adds dynamic markings, phrasings, accents, etc., in an attempt to re-create on paper what he has heard within. Three composers once told me that the performances of their music by a choir under my direction were exactly as they had hoped the music would sound. I treasure these reactions.

Interpretation is frequently equated with improving on a composer's composition. But interpretation is merely presenting the composition in as close an approximation of the composer's intention as possible WITHOUT A CONDUCTOR'S TAMPERING WITH THE SCORE. Any tampering (or "interpreting") will not increase the basic value of a composition if it is essentially a work of little worth, whereas a faithful re-creation of a work of value will heighten its significance. A bad composition will always be bad while a good composition can be masked by a misunderstanding of interpretation.

Whenever you find yourself inflating the importance of the conductor, remember that the composer can write his music and gain satisfaction even though he never hears the music performed. In fact, there are many performances of their music that composers wish they had never heard. But conductors could never conduct any music if the composer had not written it. This is not to suggest primacy of the composer, for his contribution is merely the first step toward the ultimate realization of the score in sound, for which he is dependent on others even if he conducts it himself.

Choral Music, Maestro . . . Please

When performing large choral works such as masses, ora-torios, and cantatas, the conductor should shape and scale the total performance in relation to the tone and the dynamic potential of the human voice en masse. To do otherwise does disservice to the chorus and to the music itself.

Keyboard competency is a great asset to any choral con-ductor. However, he must learn early in his career to hear vocal and choral sounds, textures, colors etc., when the hammers strike the piano strings. So frequently what appears correct (theoretically) on the printed score or is even pleasing to hear when reproduced by the piano will not sound good vocally or chorally.

Bruno Walter has referred to "the autonomous life of a piece of music,"* and as far as conductors are concerned they should borrow appropriate words from Albert Schweitzer to add "reverence" for the autonomous life of a piece of music. A conductor who is "irreverent" and feels compelled to "add his touch" to a piece of music by revising or rewriting, by altering dynamics and rhythms, etc., only succeeds in projecting his egocentricity. In re-creating any great "piece of music," a conductor must decide whether his role will be contributory or contradictory.

*Bruno Walter, *op. cit.,* p. 31.

In too many opera performances conductors forget that opera is lyric theater and conduct as if the orchestra were the focal point.

Masses of people and blobs of sound are usually demanded by conductors of "large" choral works. They are primarily concerned with quantity rather than quality. We have the post French Revolution period to thank for this emphasis on mass sound and large performing groups. Choral subtleties gave way to vocal bombardments requiring leatherized throats. The bigger the choral force, the larger the complement of instruments used by composers and demanded by conductors. And the race for dominance goes on with the composers and conductors favoring the instruments, the former by their writing (e.g. doubling the voices with brasses, poor tessituras, etc.) and the latter with their insensitivity to balance and their burying of the chorus in the rear of the stage.

Orchestral conductors spend hours learning the particular and peculiar problems involved in playing the various instruments. When they work with a choral ensemble, it is immediately obvious to a competent choral conductor that consideration of and for the human instrument has been flagrantly disregarded. The ultimate tragedy is that these conductors will never admit this defect, will never discuss it and will rarely accept help. There is one orchestral conductor whose understanding of the human voice I respect; and it is his extensive background as an opera conductor and as a superb accompanist that partially explains this depth of understanding. Toscanini and Bruno Walter worked effectively with the choral ensemble largely because of their profound respect for the human voice, yet their knowledge of choral technique from the professional standpoint could be considered "minor league." Much of their success was due to their honesty in not pretending otherwise. Many symphonic conductors today pretend, but they do not fool the singers, most people in the audience, or the orchestral personnel — only the critics. When a symphonic conductor wisely does not tamper with the preparations of a competent choral conductor, the critic hails the orchestral conductor. When he does tamper with the competent preparation (and this is usually the case), the critic blames the choral man for the poor results. When Toscanini first heard the choral work of Robert Shaw, he was immediately impressed. What was truly significant was not Toscanini's ability to recognize excellent choral work but rather his willingness to ACCEPT it and NOT tamper with it. Too many symphonic conductors today are incapable of either recognition or acceptance.

Many symphonic conductors at work today could profit from an "in depth" series of choral workshops that an authority such as Robert Shaw could provide.

Repertoire Roulette

Every time you conduct a choral concert you demonstrate for the cause of choral music. While the percentage of people in an audience capable of professional appraisal may be minimal, you must never forget that they are there. You must also care about the rest of the audience. Quality work is never wasted. The average, uninitiated listener can be excited by a top level performance just as he can be distracted by a poor performance. He may not know why he is excited or why he is distracted, but he WILL REACT.

When you limit the variety of choral repertoire you perform, you limit not only what you are able to do but also what you know.

In looking through new choral literature, do not limit your exposure to works by choral composers and arrangers already known to you. Remember that you had an initial encounter with every familiar composer and arranger. Who knows how many additional composers and arrangers might become equally familiar?

When you do not have the proper personnel to perform any of the literature you have selected, delete these works from the program. If you insist upon including these choral works you are being disrespectful to the composer, to the audience, and to the members of your choir.

A wide variety of repertoire will greatly assist the technical development of the voice and the vocal versatility of any choir provided the conductor understands style.

Future historians will probably appraise our age as a period when "interpretation" in performance superseded "re-creation," when most conductors and performers were not creatively involved as composers, when most composers were not performers or conductors, and when each area (creative and re-creative) suffered as a result.

I always prefer listening to a choir perform an easy choral work well rather than enduring a choir as it fails miserably in attempting to perform a difficult choral work.

Is the choral concert becoming a vestigial remnant? More choral groups concertize, and high school and church choirs often tour; but are the audiences as large and as interested as they used to be? Has television changed the traditional choral performance and led the public to assume that when you sing you move, dance, smile broadly, gesture, "give"? This emotive emphasis coupled with the fantastic popularity of the marching band has led me to believe that we may ultimately see and hear "marching choirs," each member wearing a lapel mike. Is it no longer possible to listen with our ears without visual interest? Has show displaced sound? Reluctance to wrestle with these questions will not avoid but merely postpone the encounter confronting every choral conductor.

Many programs are arranged so that the literature is presented chronologically. They begin with the Renaissance and move through other periods to the contemporary scene. This is but one way of programming. It is not only somewhat "old hat" but it is also the least taxing on the ingenuity of the conductor.

Repertoire should always be selected after careful consideration of the personnel. Too many conductors select for performance that music which they think they OUGHT to perform. Some are even more concerned about how their programs look in print than how they sound in performance. I once saw a most impressive printed program featuring two extended choral works. In actual performance, only one section (the easiest) of each work was actually sung. The audience might have been able to determine why, but the people who merely saw the printed program never knew why and were probably impressed by the sight but certainly not the sound. I also heard a college choir attempt to perform a Bach motet with a tenor section that would have caused me to consider seriously performing only SAB music if I had been the conductor. This programming cheats the choir out of the satisfying experience of performing repertoire within their capabilities and without exposing glaring weaknesses. Of course, they will have been exposed to Bach, but what kind of Bach? To do otherwise is much more demanding on the conductor. He must know choral literature more thoroughly. He must be willing to search, be discriminating enough to appraise what he finds, must know how and when to use this material, and must have the necessary poise for making requisite substitutions. Naturally, all of this presupposes the ability to analyze his personnel. Football coaches build their offense around their material. Too many choral conductors FORCE repertoire on their choirs.

The fast pace of life today has permeated choral activity with dangerous results. Choral conductors working with junior high school choruses choose high school and college repertoire and force their young singers to imitate singers several years beyond them in growth and development. Many high school choirs are forced by their conductors to emulate the sound of collegiate groups. Numerous college choral conductors want their choirs to sound like professional groups.

Forgotten is the fact that professional singers are mature, experienced, and technically disciplined and that the levels vary gradually to that of the beginning choir. All choral groups operate in various orbits around the choral ideal. The professional groups happen to be in a closer orbit. Of course, within each orbit there are individual groups operating at an apogee and others at the perigee of the level's potential. The athlete who can compete beyond the level of expectancy for his age is an exception. (How many baseball players began their career in the big leagues as early as Mel Ott?) So it is, or should be, in working with choral groups. Conductors have no right to expect any choral group to exceed the level or potential patent and latent at that age.

The basic reason for the existence of university choral groups is educational. Other reasons such as extra-curricular activities, recreation, and public relations are purely secondary. In spite of this, many choral conductors "use" the university choral groups. They limit the repertoire to their insular tastes. They program for the people they want to impress — friends, audiences, or prospective employers. They are more concerned about audience appeal than stylistic or technical integrity. They insist on memorization even though this limits the amount of repertoire performed during an academic year. They repeat a repertoire from one year to another as a general practice. They perform only *a cappella* music, or "pop" tunes, etc., etc., etc. To put it bluntly, THEY SHORTCHANGE THEIR STUDENTS.

Years ago, an "elder statesman" in the musical field advised me to begin every choral concert with a soft, slow work, arguing that this was the best way to attract and hold an audience. Would I agree today? No. Occasionally? Yes. One of the most stirring openers I ever programmed was Handel's *O Praise the Lord With One Consent.* Soft and slow?

Certainly not. Bold and energetic? Yes.

Perhaps the most convincing argument for the careful choice of the best choral literature for performance is that inevitably the superior quality of a choral masterwork will elevate the singer's level of involvement and the quality of his technical discipline. As a result, the composer meets the audience under favorable conditions. When this fails to happen, neither the composer nor the chorus is at fault. The conductor has failed. The ability to choose good choral literature must be augmented by the ability to guide its preparation for performance. The re-creative artistry of a chorus is dependent on the re-creative artistry of the conductor.

The excessive emphasis on attire and appearance by a growing number of choral groups suggests a new variant of "Augenmusik" since the primary impression and reaction desired are visual rather than aural. Preoccupation with sight always limits attention to sound.

A member of my choir complained about a certain choral work I planned to perform on tour. He was convinced that people would walk out on us if we sang such a piece. One night on tour, another choral conductor who arrived early for the concert was given a program and saw that we were performing this particular work. He immediately telephoned several friends, knowing of their corporate interest in this work. Moral: Who knows what interest lurks in the hearts of men?

When in doubt about how to end a festival choral concert, a safe selection is *The Battle Hymn of the Republic.* Any arrangement will do. (Were I saying this, I would have great difficulty in articulating because of the position and location of my tongue.)

Once after a concert, I had two interesting reactions. Two

people came to me and used practically the same words: "I did not know a single work which you sang tonight." Their inflections of these words told me that one was complaining because we had not sung any choral music with which he was familiar while the other was thanking me for having shared with him choral music he had never heard before. In future programming, I have always tried to remember the complaint as well as the compliment.

As an interpreter, a choral conductor must be capable of delineating the difference between spirit and emotion. The latter is more often obvious than profound and thus easier to assimilate. The former is more often elusive than peripheral and thus more difficult to assimilate.

Every conductor must work like a serious actor. The actor must lose himself in various roles or characters, and the conductor must lose himself in various styles and periods of music history.

A conductor's potential as an "interpreter" is directly related to the exposure and involvement he has had and continues to have in areas of learning other than music.

A choral conductor should have pride in his art and regard it as a mission just as a fine craftsman, painter, sculptor, or any other performing artist does. Without this posture, the best one can hope for is the casual, the routine, the uninspired, the self-satisfied, etc.

A choral conductor should have an active imagination. It should be a re-creative imagination since he must attempt to reproduce what the composer himself has previously attempted to put down in the score. It should also be a creative imagination since the stimulus of the score should arouse a dimension of artistry for which only the performers can provide a realization.

Faithfulness to a score is a conductor's prime obligation. He must reaffirm the composer's musical posture at the time the composition was written down and seek out the state of the composer's soul and spirit with empathy.

In the performance of any choral work, regardless of its style and classification, the conductor should be "arguing on behalf of the composer" in a manner that is empathetic, convincing, and contagious. To do less is to do disservice to the music, is disrespectful of one's responsibilities as a conductor, and is impossible to mask from the performers and audience. When a conductor finds it difficult to so "argue," he should assume one of two obligations: 1) he should project himself into the role of a protagonist just as an actor loses himself in a role to which he is committed; or 2) he should not perform the music.

Test any contemporary choral composition to ascertain if the composer has followed the "gesungenes Wort" principle, i.e., the words and the setting are a unified conception. This is a practice which began with Josquin des Prez and an idea which goes back to Plato. Avoid any and all choral works which clearly indicate a haphazard relationship between words and music.

Are you discouraged by the paucity of good choral publications? Being good business men, publishers are loyal to the law of supply and demand. They print what you and other choral conductors buy.

Choral conductors often consider audiences provincial in their preferences for certain choral literature and thus correctly conclude that choral concerts should be educational as well as entertaining. But never forget that choral conductors can be equally provincial and have a limited repertoire and preference. The choral conductor, however, is obligated to expand his knowledge of repertoire while the audience is not.

In the choral art, to hear is to listen, is to receive, is to appraise, is to think, is to know, is to question, is to search, is to hear, etc.

Stylistic integrity and accuracy are almost a *sine qua non* today. Choose your authority: tradition, example, research, specialist, or the unadulterated score. If you choose but ONE authority you limit the depths of your understanding.

For years I gave high credence to tradition. However, after hearing many of my former students conduct my own choral compositions (which they had sung under my direction) and detecting variable departures from the original norm, my reverence for tradition is not as great as it used to be. I also question the ultimate significance of example. It is difficult to retain accuracy in the transfer of performance practices.

Performance practices are fickle, for preferences change quickly and often imperceptibly. Aside from the excitement, wonder, and privilege, would you really enjoy hearing: Bach performing one of his cantatas at St. Thomas; Beethoven conducting one of his symphonies; Lully conducting one of his operas? The first performance? And under original circumstances? Before you answer or draw any conclusions, play some of your old recordings (tape, wire, or even disc) made earlier in your career and listen to what you once thought was good "x" number of years ago. You might be surprised, shocked, embarrassed, or (heaven forbid) even in the same rut.

The choice of choral literature for performance changes frequently and is the victim of fads. Some of these fads have been: the Russian anthem, the Negro spiritual, the folksong arrangement, the *a cappella,* anything Waring sang, the

Baroque, the contemporary, the Renaissance motet, a work which no one else has performed (unpublished or only recently published) — and now the experimental, aleatory, etc.

Preoccupation with performance of choral literature from any one given period of music history promotes a false sense of authority and of primacy and makes one tend to disregard the merit and contributions of all periods.

In the performance of standard or traditional choral literature, the conductor exercises a control related to the composer's intentions as recorded on the score. With the more recent experiments in musical composition, e.g. the aleatory, some composers do not record their intentions but merely indicate possibilities, the choice of which is to be made by the performer. Thus, the conductor is placed in a new posture which demands a different kind of decision. He can exercise no control except for an occasional and necessary "coming together" so that the improvisatory rights assigned to the performers by the composer remain inviolate. Or, he can assume more power than he has ever had before and dictate to the group what they should do with their "freedom" in performance. In either choice, neither the audience nor the composer himself will ever know what the decision actually was. Only the conductor and chorus will know.

The cult of stylistic knowledge, understanding, and integrity tends to forget that its potential significance depends not on the ability to verbalize but the ability to vocalize these concepts.

Musical paleography is significant as long as it seeks to provide an encounter with the original. However, it is dangerous when it becomes an end in itself (the worship of the written sources) and is unrelated to the manner and method of translating the original into sounds.

A choral conductor can never know enough about the past, especially the history of choral music. He should read all the research available. But he should never forget that there is a subtle difference between research and re-creation, or scholarship and performance. There is also a subtle interdependency.

.... Some choral conductors perform only the repertoire sung by their college choirs when they were in school and what that choir continues to sing.
.... Some choral conductors follow the fads and do what everyone else is doing.
.... Some choral conductors get an annual recharge from the same workshops which feature repertoire reading sessions.
.... Some choral conductors are parasitic and bleed others for repertoire ideas, suggestions, etc.
.... Some choral conductors check concert programs, reviews of new literature, reports on new releases by contemporary composers and listen to recordings.
.... Some choral conductors habitually browse among the music at convention exhibits and music stores.
.... Some choral conductors regularly scan, as much as possible, the myriad publications released each year even though they could never encounter them all.
.... Some choral conductors limit their repertoire to only one style or period, e.g. Medieval or Renaissance music, the good old days of unequal temperament.
.... Some choral conductors perform music of all styles and periods exactly the same way without any differences in performance practices.

.... Some choral conductors perform a preponderance of new music which no one else or very few others have done thereby avoiding critical analysis of performance practice.

ADD UP WHAT YOU DO AND SEE WHAT YOUR "SOME" TOTAL IS.

the finest music
LG